pebbles, debris

pebbles, debris
and other poems

* * *

Jim Dening

ARCADE
2003

First published 2003 by Arcade, an imprint of Archive Editions Ltd,
7 Ashley House, The Broadway, Farnham Common, Slough,
SL2 3PQ, UK.

A catalogue record for this book is available from the British Library.
ISBN 1840979992

Acknowledgement is made to The Rialto, South, the Bucks Free Press
and to competition anthologies in which certain poems first appeared.

In gratitude to Christopher North, whose encouragement helped the
writing of many of these poems.

Contents

Playing chess on the train to Chester

I knew what a bad move it was.
As soon as it was done I saw
each consequence unfurl until
the logic of the first entailed
the last. Before the move itself
I knew its seed was in the thought
and in the thought the error sprang
from haste and from too much desire
to press events against their grain;
while such desire in turn was born
of vanity instead of sense.

How could it matter in a game?
To press the premature attack
to push two knights up side by side
and even say that checkmate comes
in two more moves. But my son sees
beyond, and his eleven years
undo in glee my self-regard.
By accident I played my part
the difficult good father's part
that gives him life and lets me die.
How hard to give up the sweet taste
but let him taste it in my place.
He has some time before he knows
each deed is parent of the next
and long ago his end began.

Maps of the city

I used to take the black line to the centre,
travelling in the transport catacombs,
glimpsing ends of tunnels, secret rooms,
imagining the interwoven voids
of buried rivers and abandoned roads.
Rising to the surface, our memory
creates a landscape in a private code.
I used to pass a door in a familiar street;
elsewhere a window opening by a tree;
and here a room-shaped mid-air space
where once we lay, suspended in a house
long since demolished; brave explorers, we
with trembling fingers traced our bodies' lines
leading inward to the centre.

What divides, connects

This is the New World, so-called;
sitting in the Frenchtown Inn
drinking bourbon against the frost.
Outside the rushing river runs,
the desolate gray Delaware.
Imagine coming through the trees
a hundred or a thousand years ago,
hungry, fearful and without a map
unsuspecting to the river bank
and in amazement seeing this
the swirling brimming boundary
a misty quarter mile in width
and hauling past at running speed
rafts of bushes and dismasted trees.

With the rains of yesterday
the river runs engorged today
tossing its tattered detritus
beneath the trembling metal bridge.
You and I: divided, connected
by a torrent flowing through.

Enough

Between the old and new,
the yesterday and tomorrow,
the compromised, the undecided,
we ask when is enough enough,
when will we clearly know,
and choose, and move ahead
into a lighter place?
I opened my eyes, and saw
that it is enough of the old
when the leaf has fallen,
the cat has pounced,
the rain has stopped.
It is enough of the bud
when the flower comes;
but if the time for flowering passes
and there is no flower,
if the time for learning passes
but it is not learnt
then the old time is at an end,
an unknown time will take its place.

Suppose we on a winter walk
discover a diagram of change
and be, by observation, changed?

For an hour upon the Chiltern scarp
we watched the red kite climb
and sweep on empty air
as if we ourselves were empty
of bold transitions, and fed
upon amazing shapes,
until the light went off the hill,
the bird's shadow was in shadow gone,
and we, filled up with ease and clarity,
were silent after we came down.

Pebbles, debris

When two pebbles are struck together
both are damaged and not the smaller
necessarily but whichever has
an inner fault will shatter.

Stones do not grow stronger,
they endure in their compression until
by chance some shock occurs
and in unbearable tension they burst.

What good is it

What good is it when you meditate
remembering your hands and feet
and which is touching what so that
you feel grounded in the here and now – the hell
with grounded, where is the transition,
what about leaving ground behind,
when will be the subtle change?
Or do I have to pound for fifty years
dull powders like the alchemist
occasionally fired to bring together
the material and the knowledge and the heat
in case the metaphor is real
and the aspiring frustrated clay
awakes upon another level.
Now try again, be patient, wait
and watch your mantra fluttering
like a butterfly in your throat
and if you are lucky, if it is a day
with not too many itches and desires,
suddenly you are the butterfly
released in a cathedral;
you are in all the corners
and in the hands and feet,
you look down upon yourself
brave clay with strange compassion,
now you have this space this light
these shadows this knowledge
these secrets this transience
this moment.

Love for us is

Love is the slow coming, the waiting
for a week while we are apart
the exquisite purposeful journey
the moment of seeing you when time stops
and starts again and we walk slowly together
across a road, across a room;
how patient we can be, it is because
time has become as dense as fur
with close-set feelings, it is because
we have begun to make love
in the space between us and as we walk
our fingers tingle when they touch.

The day we walked the Kinder Edge

... we dressed up warm in extra layers
and marched through shallow crunching snow
with your old dog trotting and snuffling nearby
and the wind keen in our mouths and eyes;
in a semblance of shelter behind a rock we sat
sipping cognac, nibbling cake through gloves and scarves;
across stones and peat towards the clouded edge
our crumbs and words were flung away in the whistling air.

The day we walked the Kinder Edge
trudging and shivering in the wind's teeth
was a way of dancing in suspense before each other;
breathing in the mountain's eager breath,
with streaming eyes we blink and smile, knowing
beneath our layers of boots and hats and fur and fleece
we are naked, and waiting for each other, and later
your breath will flutter on my face.

Memorandum

in response to Sharon Olds

Men can be tender too
men sometimes sit on their beds next day
their mouths open in awe
thinking about how it was
when our bodies released from clothes and time
combined themselves into a single instrument
using their own secret knowledge
like trusted companions acting an old play
familiar yet newly improvised
while we watch and recognise ourselves and are amazed.

You the receiving I the penetrating
each incomplete without the other
neither knowing the other's pleasure
yet creating it together
later when we are close and full inside each other
past knowing who receives who penetrates
both interpenetrated
in a strange cathedral of private tracery
and high vaulted space
emptied of our separate desires
sensing the wisdom of our bodies
now we can be carried onward.

New words

I need new words, the leaping kind
which ought to make a difference
and bring transition from the old to new,
making what is unclear clear,
what is compromised impeccable,
what is half-felt whole-hearted
and what is shaming peaceful,
so those who hope and trust
are not disappointed or disgraced.

If we open a little door in the wall,
there is sky and light on the other side,
a rushing wind, dead leaves hurtling,
streaming backwards, forming up
and turning green before they hang once more
upon the summer oak tree on the lawn;
the sky is calm and silent now,
the old words have renewed themselves
until a cold bare season comes again.

The old path remade

Which is the better thing?
To sit and watch in evening light,
try to capture on a page
a valley filled with bright June trees
and on the further side the curving field,
the space and light and concave sky;
to take all this in at a glance
and feel it intimately infused;
then spend hours fighting words
and forget the sense of being there.

Or take a spade and spend some time
on clearing the old brick path,
cutting, pulling grass and weeds, collecting dust,
and feeling with your feet the hollow layer
where men now dead once walked
who looked from here by younger trees
towards the curving field;
until you have a path remade
sufficient for a year or two until it fades
again beneath time's weeds.

Passing ghosts

Try again walking in the street
smiling at passing ghosts
the name of god upon your lips
a few moments in the marketplace
of presence then weeks of sleep;
is this enough to prepare the way
to admit the kingdom here and now
or is it only more of the same
the dreaming the unfinished work
the coarse material unrefined;
well try again remembering
remember while you remember
from experience the rotten prospect
when higher energies slip away;
thoughts proliferate, fantasies engorge;
not just the possibility of work
not just the will to try again
but the very idea of the idea
loosens and drifts off

At Palace Wharf

The tide slides in along the river
flowing strongly in the midstream
stealthily it slithers on the mudflats
ducks and seagulls cluster closer
standing in the deepening water
until they scatter and regroup
upon another shrinking spit.

The evening falls
the river comes up close beneath the windows
it whispers and rattles in the dark
the dozing troupe of birds adrift nearby
wakes you with sudden calls
and you too sleepy to put on the light
and write down your dream:
of a strange dwelling you dreamt again
of halls and stairways and a high carved wall
with shadowed depths and spaces
frightening, comforting,
the ancient place where you belong.

The tide is going out again
you can see it at first light
strongly flowing in the midstream
uncovering the same spit and islet
for gulls' feet to imprint anew,
the half-remembered ideas of yesterday
ebbing with the river.

Chiltern diary

Here is the private landscape of desire:
abandoned bodies of the rounded hills,
half-seen untravelled depths in distant woods,
the velvet entrances, the unknown ends
of old green lanes; while curling skylines lie
upon the oblivious and alluring fields.
This closest field to home, my favourite,
begins from near the level of a man
and swells to twice the level of the trees
to make, as in this morning's morning mist,
a breathless pale horizon to the west.
I go, or in imagination go,
to pace its plump imagined middle point
and there the centre mark, to sit if dry,
to lie if hot; or in the cold today
to touch the presence of the strange domain.
Across the slope to where the oak trees grow,
now quickly scramble past the hedgerow, down
the narrowing trail between the hazel wands
and pause before the exquisite copse:
the moist and scented chamber to the field
where shadowed paths arrive and pheasants wait,
where ancient earthwork banks lie low and part
and let you pass, and rest, and be content;
then slowly homeward through the flickering light.

Pruning

It is the pruning season now,
time for cutting nature back.
Cut wisely and the plant will spring anew;
short memories of injury
replaced by promises;
in us another end of winter,
as if we ourselves made flowers grow.

With gloves and secateurs
I stand before the roses on the wall
and contemplate the complex stems,
the prickly dense enlacements,
planning to cut the oldest wood;
yet on the oldest wood
new tender tips have sprung.

I stand and wait;
wait because I cannot start,
I do not understand this plant
and don't know what to cut or leave;
so I watch, step back or talk out loud,
then cut a first few bits and look again,
and gradually I see.

I see the rose's future shape:
now I can cut the longer stems,
and create some light within;
I found a straggling stalk and on its end
a crumpled crimson flower from last year,
enfolded, beaded on the petals' rim,
now darkening and hanging down.

I cut the withered flower
and so prune myself;
the spent direction falls away,
from now the spectre of the rose renews,
another shoot will grow;
why should we fear our flower of tomorrow
will be less lovely than today?
In transformation we endure.

After 24 years at Little Hertfordshire House: preparing to leave

The bush that looks like a monkey crouching and scratching as the wind blows its leaves will be part of the forest soon if the grass is not cut around it. The climbing rose has emerged from the wild cherry's side twenty feet above the ground. Beech mast and drifting leaves assemble on the steps of the house. In the wind the front door swings. How long will the cat wait in his home if the door stays open and the fox and the owl arrive?

Now the door is closed. I will go to bed with a flashlight close at hand in case lightning trips the power. In the storm the old gutter is overwhelmed and water flows down the window pane. The oak sill is hollowed to its heart. After the rain moonlight moving on the bedroom wall turns into summer dawn. I have opened the window to smell the air and hear the first birds. Down the lane still runs a rivulet, carrying mud and twigs away.

Waking

This morning, leaning on the garden gate,
how idly you could watch the world outside,
reflecting safely on the rush-hour tide
and waving to the lingerers, and the late.
How snugly, smugly then you turned around,
when suddenly you felt the gate's hard edge,
heard the loud robin scratching in the hedge,
observed the moss-grown pebble on the ground,
and smelt a wisp of biting bonfire smoke.
Tasting the morning's presence in the air
you saw, because another sense awoke,
yourself as if a stranger standing there.
The inner and the outer worlds are one;
but even as you look, the moment's gone.

Communion

I was raising a glass of wine –
not to see the crimson light –
it was in a corner of the kitchen –
not to mark a feast with friends –
it was an odd time of day –
not to celebrate some great event –
it was my usual village wine –
when by chance I remembered
(perhaps by chance, but there is
a calendar in our unconscious part)
that today is my father's birthday,
and twenty years ago he didn't make
his birthday by about six hours,
the evening before, peacefully, in the end.
Avidly I drink this small communion,
in remembrance, in continuation,
and as the wine courses, I imagine
his blood flowing in my veins.
His window was open, there was a blue sky,
you could hear birds chirping in the bushes,
it seems to be the same today; perhaps
it is always like this on a fine August evening
when your senses are concentrated
and something important has happened after all.

The fleeting small hours

Do you lie watching
through the interminable
the fleeting small hours
staring at darkness
your old eyes unfocussed
seeing not understanding
glimpses of light from somewhere else
at the end of a silver cord they say
or the corridor outside your room
or the moon torn from earth's rib
reflecting the night time edges of our lives
and your night full of mists
the memories of Gwen and Doris
and holidays in Bruges outside you now
drifting off in space
details sometimes caught by others
me for example reminding you
of things you used to talk about
of pleasant moments in your life
if you can hear me

The quiet mother

Age has robbed your knowledge of yourself
it robs us all of clarity and intent
though usually in merciful degrees
allowing wit or rage to mock it yet
but you old mother you depend on me
to mock on your account the incapacity
that stole on you and waits perhaps for me.

The friends who knew you once
if they were near enough to watch
and young enough to live till now
tell me how marvellous you were
for me your child to you closebound
you sang the song of a mermaid down
at the bottom of the deep blue sea
and you still fresh in motherhood
suggesting other possibilities
another woman I never knew
available for a transient spell
perhaps but long since drowned.
You put an undemanding self
at the disposal of the world
to make things nice for us or them
they always they were in authority
as if the aim were to behave in class
and have your mourners at your grave
say ee but she was good.

Now in weakness you forget the best
you murmur that it's not all right
you forget your quality and worse
you forget the reasons for your life
you could not share the history you hid
you never spoke about your parents' death
within a year and you fifteen years old
this was the vital robbery of yourself
what real part shrank or suddenly was sealed
what hollow game of strength have you sustained
till now it flees away to join its source.
Before you die I wait and speak of things
so that you hear my voice as if your father's voice
and hold your hand in mine as if your father's hand.

Shaking weeds

Weeding in my father's garden
beyond the corner of the lawn,
feeling soil in bare-toed sandals,
shaking weeds in bunches.
Along the long hoe handle
another robin squints at me,
thinner, younger than his fathers
thirty years before him.

This one comes up close and flutters.
he doesn't know who I might be;
finds the stranger half familiar
as the weeds are shaken,
in the way I rest half-standing
fore-arms leant on bended knees,
grunt when reaching further forward,
whistle at the robin.

Then the boy's eyes always followed
the father's hands upon the soil,
couldn't see the autumn shadow
spreading in the garden.
Robin vanished, weeding finished,
we set off for the proper call;
held my father's feeble fingers,
felt them, shook them gently.

It creeps up on you

The original khaki donkey jacket
big pockets and a flap to button up the collar
lined with stuff like army blanket
once my father's wartime motor cycle coat,
I adopted later as noble and inspiring gear
on my erratic Royal Enfield, falling off
in gratitude inside its padded shoulders.
This coat, one-time defender of the realm,
clung for years to shreds of honour while it faded
under falling leaves towards its battered state,
attacking only bonfires on winter afternoons.
Not long ago, and not the same exhausted coat
but its spiritual heir, another tatty jacket,
my daughter borrowed for a country walk
and said: – hey, Dad: the same things are always
in the pockets of your gardening coat;
there are various bits of string ...
– Ah, twine, say I, you never know, twine is useful
in a garden. – And the rest! says she,
a stubby pencil and a crumpled notebook ...
– Of course, say I, in a garden you never know,
a poem might come up in an unexpected place.
– And then, said Sophie, there was a smooth round pebble
and a brownish hanky that smelled of you.
I fell silent, remembering after my father died
I burnt his papers and useless things on a bonfire
at the bottom of my childhood garden
and in his gardening jacket found a pebble
and a brownish hanky that smelled of him.

In the cathedral

Taking your step forward, you were singing
at the edge of light; while I in darkness
by the furthest pillar listening, nervous, blissful,
full of confidence and ignorance,
aware of the difficult high requiem
approaching inexorably as a birth;
and you preparing the successive platforms
of your voice to bear up the quiet word.
The moment comes and is transformed.
The voice ascends among the solid piers
vanishing in darkness at the vault,
visiting dim alcoves and forgotten saints,
inspiring the stony fabric, persuading
the spirit of the place to leave its echo
hanging in the air. Beside my fluted column,
from an unseen source a ray of light descends
and makes a spot of colour on the ground.

The cherry tree
In memoriam Dieter Schiek, d.1997

*[A cherry tree sometimes puts on a great show of fruit the year
before it dies, in an instinct of self-propagation. It is only
obvious in retrospect.]*

Where only the stump remains
among the living trees
last year we saw the cherry tree
laden with its coming death
bent beneath the heavy fruit of yesterday
stuffed with sweetness
its branches so curved beneath the weight
the cherries of the air descended to the ground
to become earth again
and the white stones all round
were stained with their juice.

We saw you among us last year
you who without knowing knew
you would not bear again tomorrow's fruit
and now we see
the actions of your life are still traced out
around the vanished trunk
the fruit of your love
remains without decay
the white stones of memory
come by themselves at night
to shelter your dust.

Ode to fire

after – a long way after – Pablo Neruda

Before the fire
the cat stretched out
warms your foot
with a rough tongue
be careful lest
the cat writhes
and scratches
small flames
seek holds
diffidently
on cold wood
at first
they will not
burn you
orange fingers
capriciously
amorously
grasp their logs
behind and round
now the flames
are writhing
wood is become
a snowy landscape
you can look at
but not touch
unless to walk upon
barefoot
now the flames
make water boil
blood boil

the bread is risen
the loaf half made
the martyr
half consumed
the pupil observes
elements seethe
in the crucible
sparks whisk
in the chimney
seconds whisk
years whisk
smoke rises
in still air
small birds soar
on warm draughts
sprinkling ashes
beside an oak
I was amazed
how gritty
the residue
I have seen
hollow forms
of men and dogs
petrified in ash
I have ordered
my body's ordeal
by fire
whereas wit
shall be preserved on paper
until consumed in turn.

Over there the light

Over there the light
shrinking in the western sky
down into low trees
at the far river side
and the pale pathway
over rippled water
breaking and confused
running out in shadows;
over here the mud
the absurd tangle of branches
repellent remnants
of tidal rubbish.

In the morning I went down
to look for strange shapes of wood
along the river shore
and there I found cast up
and damaged on the gravel
a small carved statue of a god
with many arms
now retrieved and in my house
although not understood
and I uncertain if I have the right
or if the influence is good.

Now light is on this side until tonight
the tide has swept the river clean
and joined its distant banks again.

Pushing off from the shore

Pushing off from the shore
floating and waiting near the bank
still in shallow water just within
almost within reach of solid ground
whimsically turning end on end
taken by a swirl of current
steadily proceeding further out
to where the surface heaves
and waves uplift you
where you knew fear once
above the void
until the element which bears you
strongly drifting sweetly breathing
brings you to another place
lapped by calmer water
an island refuge or could it be
the further shore.

If we are lucky

If we are lucky in the middle of our lives
there is a tranquil plateau; never mind
the financial pressure which unremits
or the private pain which intermits.
There is a time when you though crazed
(remember crazed is to be blessed
and blessed has special pleasures such
as gravely acknowledging a cat
or seeing how strange are people on the street)
when you though crazed are in your mind
and they your children are grown in theirs.
This is the juncture from one life to another
and the best connection you can make beyond
the warm assembly leading to their birth.

We are the revolutionaries

… we risk our families and our peace of mind
and in a small way our good name as if we care
that which is hidden of our desires we reveal
we dissemble to our friends and worse
we lie to those who trusted us before
we know we guard our secrets till our deaths
we have seen betrayals of people who confide
desperate to ease loneliness or be approved
who cares about trivial deceits in a great cause
but what if the cause is trivial
and the deceits are great
we think all is justified we are swept along
by necessity and force of will
we ignore persistent doubt
what barricades? what fine defiance?
what direction? toward the fire or toward the ashes?
we are the revolutionaries
the revolutionaries of love
the banal revolutionaries of love
we are the adulterers.

Another road

It was a long haul upward through the trees
along a heavy track aligned
on far imagined compass points,
often travelling in a gloom
of heavy evergreen, peering curiously
up other sidelong forest tracks,
cheered by sudden glimpses
over a sunstrewn valley and glinting water.
This dogged journey was in the time
of strength and clarity, the middle years;
always the idea of home lay close at hand,
with children's voices and glowing windows.

I wake, and realise the road so-called
is rough and sharp and ill-defined
and has been so for quite some time;
the ghosts of children's voices calling
are behind me now and faint;
the way ahead is blocked with boulders,
the day is fading, birds have hidden in the trees.
I look behind, and see, or seem to see
the road I followed turning back into a path,
past where it bent in the undergrowth,
and in uncertain leaf-veiled shade,
the hidden turning to another way.

I would go back, but when I turn
the track and all that is behind are blurred;
I will dive aside, scrambling
down the gulley and through the ferns
to join up with where the other path was going.

As if I could; as if it were so near.
At nightfall in old stories
candles are lit in windows
and wolves begin to howl;
before it is too late I am crashing down
through rocks and brambles, determined
to find the way continuing in failing light.

Waiting by the door
(after Kafka)

What should we learn in this life anyway?
None of the useful or professional things
such as polishing a table or a sentence.
Where is the doorway to another level,
where is the stairway, even the first step?
The hard-earned knowledge will slip away
and be extinguished on the final day
save fragments passed to half-heeding children
for them to store and spend and lose in turn.
There is a granary of souls supposedly,
and ways of working against the grain
to slip between the cracks of the gross world.
The door is here; you have only to open it
and pass through. The door is here; you have only
to open it and pass through. Oh deceptive faith,
we wait, and wonder why we are not changed,
we spend a lifetime searching for the subtle access,
like dogs sniffing at gateways all along the road.

The same river

You have a single time to do
each thing you choose or chooses you.
This seemed not so when we were young.
We expected second chances for tomorrow,
we would return one day before the Sacré Coeur,
and stand unchanged upon the Pont des Arts.
I still took care to walk symmetrically
up stairways and across the squares
avoiding lines and touching things in turn:
the homesick anxious child repelling death.
The boy knew dimly whose mortality
accompanied him around the monuments
and stood beside him at the parapet,
in moments gazing at the Mona Lisas,
trying to memorise elusive smiles
while lives pass by and friends move on.

Go again to the river, and lean upon the bridge,
stare down and fix upon a piece of debris
as it drifts beneath and down the stream.
Dive in and bring it back, arrest its moment,
or like the dog you are, run barking down the path
as the random twig is borne away and disappears;
scurrying flotsam, empty of attention. Not the twig:
you, me.

Disqualified

I used to think the ordinariness
of a calm loving upbringing in a village
with a by-pass through its middle,
an army camp, a zoo and mental hospital
beyond the cabbage fields and the canal,
hearing lions roaring and monkeys howling
in the western part of Cheshire
close to holidays in Wales;
with parents known to those who saw them
for riding a huge old bicycle
and winning the fruit cup every year
or being the village librarian on Tuesdays
and secretary of the WI;
homegrown beans and lettuce on the table
and never a voice raised in anger;
I used to think such ordinariness,
such orderliness, such security
should disqualify a grateful child
from also feeling puzzlement or pain.

Poetry feels like

Poetry is not delicate sentiments
nervously expressed and avoiding offence,
poetry feels like what is going on here,
impatient feelings and the search for words,
the incomprehension of things, the transient attention,
the arguments and the competitive people
who can do better. Politely we listen
to the sensitive new voices,
give us your gossamer but let it be
hot and strong and bind bodies together,
we want delicate which whacks you,
we want our desire to accord with yours,
we want words which mate together,
feeling our sex on our sleeves' edge,
looking at the world with puzzled faces,
remembering the pain of others,
expressing expectation strongly.
Otherwise what is it worth,
it is like having a cup of tea
and much nodding with parents' friends
or talking of our life's desires
with the beloved mother who wants
who wanted to have felt such things herself
all those years ago and is afraid
to grant them to her child
in case he gets hurt.

Empty plunging

You can understand impatient people
with their tapering glances
and unfinished sentences
pistols in handbags
desperate gulping of stuff

there is no point in
enumerating absurd things
the train which overran the buffers
and pokes through the end of the station
hanging down into the street

better to smile with friends
murmuring ah
at sleeping children
that's what we are
with our ears sticking out

otherwise it is empty plunging
and the plumage of the scrawny
and conspiracy breathing inside
a punctured plastic bag
and exhaustion

please wait until tomorrow
I ought to have a bath
and get dressed and ready
it takes a long time
I prefer being naked

Sonata form

There they are again,
the muffled hammer blows,
and a noiseless noise
continuing;
I got out of bed
in the small hours to see
if there was work going on
nearby in the dark,
how absurd!

Stepping outside later
for a walk
for some peace
from things inside,
the wind rushes at my ears;
if I turn one way
the air is flat and silent,
the other way and I receive
a buffeting fugue
of invisible forms.

After the opening
so-called hammer blows,
among the variations
silence waits;
sounds seek their places
in the silence,
new structures follow,
melodies develop,
sometimes
the intermittent rhythm
reappears.

Detuned

I was in the middle of a poem
a different one from this
though it is happening again now
thinking about half written things
detuning my mind to let in new words
suddenly there is something going on
voices spaces shapes dim movements
I am not alone inside
there is nothing obvious to be seen
if I look hard like in the street
but if casually I inspect
with a sideways corner glance
stalking in the spaces of the world
shadows figments slip away from view
like unlived possibilities or if I listen
not minding car noises or the typing
slivers and odd lumps of sound arise
and tremble until they drip away
not heard so much as felt
the fragmented realm continues
its obscure comforting company
of people or features or parts of people
their characters and ideas unknown
apparently but suggestive
and the objects the world's objects
circulating behind their screen
intermittent hints of other orders
like running the dial past radio stations
and tuning in only to find
snatches of a strange language.

The Bokhara boil

What sickness or idea
congests the face
confuses the mind
while round the limbs
the inhabitant migrates
forcing up a lump
in the lump are both
the sickness and its cure
of parasite and host
which is better for the world
which is virtuous
which is sacrificed?
hating the infesting poem
deliver it through revulsion
remember how
surgeons cut and pinch
secure the end
or the beginning
draw it slowly forth
not breaking segments
not losing the thread
wrap it round the pencil
les vers visqueux s'enroulent
autour du crayon
is it worth the trouble
suppose it breaks
the rest darts back
infects the system longer
even if you get it out
unbroken what good is it
you lay it on the table
revolting and useless

Washing radish

Washing radish in the sink
I have a system for nipping off the radish tail
with a swift thumb nail
and depositing the nipped bit to one side
in a pile of tails
while separating the radish proper
with the same thumb nail
from the supermarket rubberbanded clutch
of stinging radish leaves
and dropping the plump red white-tipped French
breakfast radish
breakfast?
radish in cold water to be washed.
This goes superbly well for six or seven
radish until I realise
I have dropped a radish out of sync
among the rubbish tails.
Smiling humbly at this foible I repair
the deft routine
and even then I drop another
bloody radish wrong
because of thinking of the system.
Smiling differently I am watching
the division of attention
when helplessly a third radish
drops upon its tail
completing the lesson, and like a child
I stop and redirect my hands and start again
wondering if things are normal
or something radical required.

South Bucks, May 1997

Oh! the wry faces in our village
after election night.
Living there twenty years, assuming
from a sort of Christianity
and well-meaning humankind
that we were of the same community,
I said to certain friends
with a perfectly sincere air,
aren't you happy now?
It is a new dawn is it not?
and watched their faces crumple.
Oh! the satisfaction.
How we laughed,
with Dick and Penny
the only two others more or less
and my little family
and our two cats,
how we laughed.

A few days later
at a publisher's party
in Islington naturally
nobody I met had been to bed at all
upon election night
(and these are people who go to bed
rather than not)
which tells you that something in life
is better than sex.
Something like what?
Justice? Equality? A strange sense
of deliverance from servitude?
No wonder we laughed, with all that by dawn
and sex not used up yet.

Early morning women

Towards nine o'clock along the street
the early morning women are streaming by
look at this one the bright face tells you
the wet hair the whirl of fragrance
she is one of the early morning women
only a few moments out of the shower
those few moments ago
she was drying between and underneath
powdering the moist bits
perfuming her neck
and moments before that
sliding out of her warm bed!

You shameful voyeur you man
you fantasist how can you pursue
this unwarranted invasion why
this woman could have slept chaste
or by preference on her own
or have scrambled beans on toast
for children before school
or made the feared hospital appointment
or disgraced her partner with disdain
or eked out a lonely night in misery
and all of these unfit for prurient regard.

But some are glistening like voles in sunlight!
they want you to know how they feel
and how marvellous it is
the bolder ones are striding out
the quiet dreamy-eyed ones
are still trembling inside
don't try to meet their eye
just mind your own business
and look forward to tomorrow.

Trick a new person

Better sex more money less tax
exude confidence enjoy life
to the full crammed full live longer
look great in passport photos
know why smokers have smaller penises
get free food free land free holidays
get pregnant standing on your head
reduce puffiness bags and wrinkles
trick a new person into liking you
buy a tv for £5 flee baldness blight
eliminate depression and self-doubt
dental fillings can make you ill
always get the best seat on planes
best day of month to buy a car
most people haven't got a clue
how to choose or serve champagne
add a woman's pubic hair to fishing bait
win spot the ball competitions
what to do if your urine turns green
get top of range cameras at half price!
know what people are thinking about you
touch this spot on your body to switch off
find a long lost friend or relative
don't lose your teeth to mystery disease
know where to find the cheaper pint
discover the price of everything
and a human being who will love you
even though you are rich popular successful
wise clairvoyant unwrinkled
with lots of teeth and hair
numerous tv sets and cameras
a remarkable set of genitalia
and no idea what to do next.

Knowing, not knowing

There are always things you didn't know
and when you know them
it seems to make a difference.
How often in the paper we read a thing
and think I'm glad I know that,
glad I'm living now, otherwise
if I were dead I wouldn't know.
I start feeling sorry for my poor old dad
now dead and hasn't read the papers recently
brought up like me believing
in the principle of progress, namely
every discovery is a revelation
every invention an improvement
additions to knowledge are
additions to civilisation
therefore living now is better than before.
There is something wrong with this idea.

The universe got bigger yesterday
the reaches of the Milky Way are full of ice
rocks older than previous oldest rocks are found in Canada
dinosaurs are not extinct but hop about like robins
chimpanzees are self-aware and count to nine
genome project offers human blueprint
Gulf Stream may reverse its flow
Stonehenge is earlier than we thought and built by Gauls
a four hundred thousand year old spear
forces rethink on first humans
the Dead Sea scrolls decoded
force rethink on the crucifixion
this seems worth knowing though

no one told us it before.
What foolish questions shall we ask
the great men of the past and what they knew
or didn't need to know.
Oh Montaigne, oh Shakespeare, Goethe,
oh ironists, collectors of absurdities,
did you die thinking ruefully you didn't know
the things by chance the later people know?
There is something wrong with this idea.

We the later people, or we the people born
before later later people such as
our children or our children's children,
only know our little accidental swathe.
I saw today more news of refugees,
five hundred died of cholera last month.
Is this worth knowing? Is this progress?
Things which do not change flow
in a stream, what our decent fathers knew
we have to learn again and share with them.
You may as well decide at any time
there is what you know and what you don't,
it makes no difference as to how things are.
Just as well since new important matters
and bound to force a rethink
will be discovered on the day you die
and of no consequence to you at all.

Indifference

Every day
we look in the mirror those of us
who have a mirror
to shave or adjust our expression.
We see the old familiar face. In full summer
when the trees were heavy I said to you:
at the same time every day let us take a picture
of the oak tree.
Then we will see it progressing through the year.
How will we take the same shot each time?
Stand in the same place, if it rains or snows
it will prove the differences of the days.
This sounds like a good idea! We will make
a book of photographs, like films we have seen
speeded up of flowers blooming in five minutes
or a mouse devoured by insects to the bone.
We will see this great tree in splendour
reduced to
a wintry
skeleton,
yet from
day to day
you never notice any difference, do you?

At the Fontaine de Vaucluse

When you arrive beneath the wall
look up slowly, the eye takes time
to assimilate such verticality,
lean against a rock in case
you feel dizzy and fall over –
the cliff beetles outward, reflecting
in reverse the illusion in King Lear
with halfway up the dots of shrunken birds
and imagined samphire clinging to the vein;
entire realms of nature stratified
in leaning rooms and overhangs,
shadowed grottoes smoothed by waves
that fell back thirty million years ago;
shrubs scrabbling toe holds kicking dust
and at the very rim miniatures of trees
jut against the sky. With map and compass
others may see the unimaginable
and explore the upper sphere
peering fearfully beyond
the crumbling lip; not us,
we are poised upon a stepping stone
between the worlds.

The mountain is full of water
as if a heaving chamber pressing
in the rock beside you;
not just this cliff – the whole system
back to the Ventoux twenty miles
and the Alps beyond, filtering,
sifting, settling, indeed they say
the flow into some other hole has taken

two thousand years to percolate,
the length of Christianity
equal to a drop of water.

In the dry season the abyss appears,
unwisely you can scramble round
on slippery boulders darkening
into the waiting gullet;
the river starts way down its bed
seeping out of rocks.
With the melting of the snows
imagine the waters swelling,
filling the blind reservoirs
until beneath the cliff
the level rises into light
covering the boulders
where once you stood
filling out to the wall
sucking the roots of trees
flat and pallid yet
little swirls flickering
the mass moving inside itself
the heap of water bulging
and at the rim at last
surging over the rocks
in a thick purling wave
leaping out and away
like a grey panther
smooth and violent
close and tempting,
dangerous, dispassionate,
all the strangeness of it
washed out from those caverns.

The ghosts of Canons Ashby

I: on the mound

On a bitter day I set out across the field
to visit my old neighbours over there,
to walk where they had led their lives
and listen for whispers and dim echoes:
my neighbours of five hundred years ago
who left the banks and hollows of their village
smoothing out beneath the centuries of sheep;
and ancient neighbours who were there before,
the ones I cannot visualise, nor imagine
two millennia year by year, and they so unafraid
of prolonged colossal labour, or so coerced,
they raised ten thousand waggon loads of soil
within concentric rings of dowser energy
to make a flat round mass of fifty yards across;
now eroded, now grown upon with leaning pines,
but high, and solid, and deliberate.

On the mound's edge, checking with cold fingers,
thinking the top must be a neutral space,
I found the pendulum turned suddenly,
and on the farther edge it turned again;
with the shock of recognition, I saw
the church tower as if waiting to be seen,
fixed upon a suggestive unseen line
by old tradition in the rightful place.

I would invite these neighbours for a drink;
I will revise my early English primer

and show my book of druid ceremony,
and gaze at them and listen and enquire
just how they measured and what they knew,
whether they had a science of the earth
which we ignore, and if they lived along
the dim vestigial tracks beside my house,
and – to make me tread more gently –
where their bodies lie. But if they spoke
I might hear old anger and discomfort,
the suffering of drudgery and disease,
the servile centuries of ploughing strips,
the fear of dark and dispossession.
Whether I ask or not, there are no voices;
Their ghosts are far off and will not come.

II: borrowed eyes

Shivering, attentive, naked at the window
I watched a silver dawn arriving in the park,
uncovering the night's frost and sending mists
to shrivel on the downward slope;
the oak trees, leafless, knotted with centuries,
in the new light were pink and delicate,
and on their shadowed side, quite black.
Not a twig, nor blade of grass, nor wisp
of sheepswool moved, except the fur of frost
escaped across the grass before the sun
and a chaffinch sidled on the lilac branch.

Well, I saw all this with borrowed eyes.
Not my gaze, not my half-awakened body
just out of bed, not even my own feelings;

but an old vision seen through other eyes
and an old sense before an older day.
The ghost is in the glance through this same window
at a fine frosty dawn, and then with precious little time
for admiration before the work began.
From nearby dwellings a thousand years ago
early they went to plough the ridge and furrow
which shines this morning in the flattened sun;
five hundred years ago, to plant the oaks,
suddenly no longer pink but rough and live.
My borrowed eyes I will pass on in trust
for future souls to use, five hundred or
a thousand years from now, when frost will glint
and young oaks glimmer in the morning light.

III: at the village

The hollow way is flooded now; this was
the old main street, a sunken lane,
inviting thoughts of unknown centuries
of feet or hooves or wheels that cut its track.
The modern road, laid on a side alley,
has filled across and dammed the upper part.
I have found the nearest to a village map,
a historian's sketch of banks and ditches
with fine lines of spidery wedges
running in curves and shaded swoops,
opening out around the dwelling spaces,
clustering along the sharp indented runnels.
The main thoroughfare is like a creature's bowel,
rounded, organic, with arteries and nerves
spreading towards the village edge.

From the centre, beside the hollow way,
you can see the empty manor house and church;
I count the former dwellings in the field:
one ledge and then a ditch; two and then a ditch;
but slopes become confused with refuse holes,
the centuries are overlaid and shapes are lost.
I am walking through the midst: not politely
up an ancient path between the plots, but straight
across boundaries, through walls, through homes,
through people. All this in my time, not in theirs;
thus are ghosts removed by a dimension,
and I shall be as solid as they are now.
Formerly the arrow, firebrand, plague
flew through their doors and bodies;
the charitable priory enclosed the acres,
two thousand sheep ran upon the ruins.
Now the summer grass is long, the banks
and ditches are disguised. One small voice
is heard among the empty places of the park,
and a fresh wind blows above the village mounds.

IV: at the church

If the shape reflects the spirit
there is curtailment in the church,
a loss of purpose. Beyond the altar,
outside the sudden eastern wall
an oblong mound continues
the church's width for fifty yards;
like a wreck devoured by sand,
low, flattish, lumpy, half grazed upon,
a few dismasted tombstones leaning down.

The black friars at their mattins gape
as the blurred figure of a man
dressed in strange colours and inventions,
bald head, glasses, talking to himself,
emerges from the wall, treading air,
stumbles and pauses at the chancel steps,
studiously paces to and fro, and passes through
without disturbing them the waiting bread and wine,
not hearing the trembling plainsong,
not seeing the fearful signs of the cross.

Near the flat mound's end,
before the boundary yews,
a hidden spring will show
where the old altar stood.
Dissolution brings dissolution:
from the bare ruined choir
stones with a rich patina
of prayer and prejudice
have flown across the road
and are become stair and cellar,
kitchen, office, bedroom, bookroom.

A roadside scene

Where the road turns sharply down
the camber slopes the wrong way
trees shroud the hill on both sides
the surface is rough and slippery.

A man is picking his way along the edge
the rain makes tears on his face
trucks are looming up beside him
it is not a good time to be doing this.

It is never a good time at this corner
the downward cars go swishing by
he takes old flowers from the broken fence
on the last post he hangs a new bouquet.

He hears an engine howling nearer
sees it leaning for the corner
sees the front wheel slide away
the bike cascading in a flash of sparks.

He stands foursquare with arms outstretched
catches the somersaulting body of the boy
oh, they go flying but he has him
he has him and he holds him safe.

By all the miserable roadside shrines
wait memories with outstretched arms
calling names in desperate whispers
shuffling through the withering flowers.

Like the Orinoco

Face pressed to the ground
eyes closed short hair
red and green shirt
his football team perhaps
chosen that morning
for the event
his hand clenched
as if he had tried
desperately
to suck his thumb
and beneath his head
reaching into the dust
a dull red river system
like the Orinoco
seen from on high.

On one hand or the other

I

All the precision of a military operation,
some of it witnessed on national television,
was brought to bear on the saving
of Joseph Hoskins' right hand yesterday.

A neighbour brought the unlucky victim
of a farming accident fainting to a garage
where in moments a trucker, an ambulance and finally
an air force helicopter rushed him to hospital.

Meanwhile police searched the scene of the accident
and the severed hand was brought packed in ice
to the hospital where in six hours of microsurgery
it was painstakingly reattached. Later on TV

the surgeon said the hand should be able to grasp again
and the patient, while tired, thanked people for their help.

II

All the precision of a medical operation,
some of it witnessed on national television,
was brought to bear on the severing
of Yusuf Al-Hussein's right hand yesterday.

The police brought the luckless victim
of a neighbour's denunciation fainting to a courtroom
where in moments, despite his denials, a cleric
sentenced him for stealing a farmer's lamb.

The TV showed the aftermath of the operation
in a flickering image of a bloodless hand
exhibited separately on a table,
its bones and fragmentary ends exposed.

The patient lay morosely grasping his loss,
with a bandaged stump to encourage the others.

Throwing stones

When you are walking in a country lane,
                    and pick up a round stone
and feel its comfortable weight upon your palm,
                    and take it home,
or hide it at the seventh pace beyond the post,
                    or throw it in the air,
remember that just now another man
                    picked up another stone somewhere

and feels its weight within his hand,
                    it needs sufficient weight,
and then will roll his sleeve, and look around,
                    and spit, and shout,
he under the same sun of woman born,
                    he your brother, he your counterpart,
like you he does what he has learnt
                    and what he believes is right.

Beliefs arise from accidents of birth,
                    and from causes not our own
our actions flow; even while you reason this
                    his stone has flown,
the latest in the ghostly hail that
                    violent history has strewn
on dogs and men; and now not you,
                    by chance, but he has thrown

this round and pleasing stone of yours
                    upon an unknown woman's head
enshrouded in a clean white sack, her body buried,
                    and in the name of god.

Below the surface

Hurt eats away at you like corrosion
ate the subframe and door sills
of the old car sitting in the yard,
we had plates welded over the decay.
How about hacking off the plates
and submerging the wreck
in salt water to be cleansed?
Then curious and oblivious fish
will swim through clean, but dead, bones.

There are ways of dealing wisely
with deep old injuries aching
from anger or belittlement.
By all means hack off the plates
but submerge the wreck in oil,
in almond oil with fragrant herbs
and lavender in a bowl nearby
wine trembling in a glass
and a friend laying on hands
to bring one bruise, at least, to the surface.

Another life

I dreamt I woke into another life,
where we lived not in the middle
but at extremities of time and place,
on different levels, where we watched
forests spring up and rivers carve their beds,
seas and mountains changing places;
or our eyes became so quick, we saw
lightning hanging in the air,
a bullet revolving as it flew,
an incandescent particle defer
its moment of bursting into flame.
Through caves and cellars we saw below
the ground, with dim abandoned forms
and rotten stairs and pitch black holes;
we gazed towards the dazzling sky,
where once the gentle prophets dwelt,
and found it flowing down upon us
into the airless clasp of earth and dark.

The people are streaming in the street,
when the rain falls or the sun appears
they turn their faces upward, how touching
to see their trust and aspiration, not knowing
the light must be eclipsed again.
Loving fathers will sacrifice
themselves to save their sons,
women will gather children round
to shield them with their bodies.
They hope to wake into another life,
rising from the warm earth,
trees rich in autumn colours,
insects busy in the grass.

Looking back

We were out in rough country
the other day where the whole time
we had to walk with heads down,
watching where to put each foot
on muddy stones and tufts.
We would stop for breath
and slowly raise our heads
so as not to lose our balance,
then look back along the track.
How far we've come, how high –
a buzzard glides beside us.
The wind chants across the holes
in the old stone wall; coming nearer
across the tops we seem to see
the old musician striding out,
flute to his lips, ancient faced,
always starting his journey again,
bridal flowers beneath his heel,
looking ahead, always looking ahead.